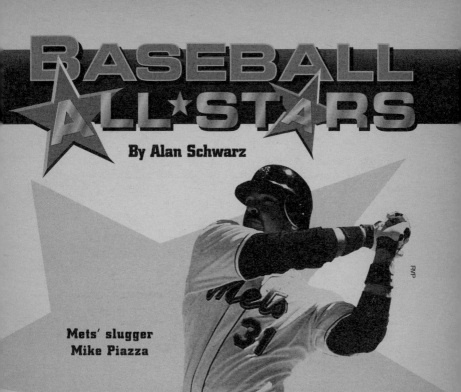

BASEBALL ALL★STARS

By Alan Schwarz

Mets' slugger
Mike Piazza

A *Sports Illustrated For Kids* Book

Baseball All-Stars by Alan Schwarz
A SPORTS ILLUSTRATED FOR KIDS publication/November 1999

SPORTS ILLUSTRATED FOR KIDS and **KiDS** are registered trademarks of
Time Inc.

Cover design by Emily Peterson Perez
Front-cover photographs by Tom DiPace (Sammy Sosa) and Greg
Abramowitz/Sports Imagery (Ken Griffey, Junior)
Back-cover photograph by Tom DiPace (Mike Piazza)
Interior design by Nina Gaskin

Baseball All-Stars is published by SPORTS ILLUSTRATED FOR KIDS, a division of Time
Inc. Its trademark is registered in the U.S. Patent and Trademark Office and in
other countries. SPORTS ILLUSTRATED FOR KIDS, 1271 Avenue of the Americas,
New York, N.Y. 10020

For information, address: SPORTS ILLUSTRATED FOR KIDS

ISBN 1-886749-73-6

Printed in the United States of America

10 9 8 7 6 5 4 3 2 1

Baseball All-Stars is a production of SPORTS ILLUSTRATED FOR KIDS Books:
Cathrine Wolf, Assistant Managing Editor; Emily Peterson Perez, Art Director;
Amy Lennard Goehner and Margaret Sieck, Senior Editors; Sherie Holder and
Michael Northrop (Project Editor), Associate Editors; Nina Gaskin, Designer;
Kathleen Fieffe, Reporter; Robert J. Rohr, Copy Editor; Erin Tricarico, Photo
Researcher; Ron Beuzenburg, Production Manager

Contents

Introduction

Big-league baseball is full of big-time stars. There are veteran performers, young guns, and World Series wonders. There are home-team heroes and colorful characters from across the country. With so many *stars*, it's not always easy to say who's best. And that's where *we* come in!

Baseball All-Stars is your guide to the very best players in baseball. We've looked at each league, American and National, and selected the top player at each position. It wasn't easy! We picked some players, such as pitchers Pedro Martinez and Randy Johnson, because they're simply *overpowering!* We chose others, such as Ivan "Pudge" Rodriguez and Roberto Alomar, because they are defensive wizards.

We've even saved some space for Honorable Mentions, the athletes who didn't quite make our starting lineup. *Baseball All-Stars* includes the names you know, like veteran super-sluggers Mark McGwire and Sammy Sosa, as well as the game's rising young players. Check out these new faces in our Stars of the Future chapter. And in our Tribute chapter you can read about a pair of baseball legends — Cal Ripken, Junior, and Tony Gwynn.

As you can see, this book has more starpower than most galaxies. So read on to find out which ones shine the brightest, and why we think these 41 men deserve to be called *Baseball All-Stars.* ★

American League Starting Lineup

RHP	Pedro Martinez, Boston Red Sox
LHP	David Wells, Toronto Blue Jays
RP	Mariano Rivera, New York Yankees
C	Ivan Rodriguez, Texas Rangers
1B	Mo Vaughn, Anaheim Angels
2B	Roberto Alomar, Cleveland Indians
3B	Travis Fryman, Cleveland Indians
SS	Alex Rodriguez, Seattle Mariners
OF	Ken Griffey, Junior, Seattle Mariners
OF	Juan Gonzalez, Texas Rangers
OF	Manny Ramirez, Cleveland Indians
DH	Jose Canseco, Tampa Bay Devil Rays

PEDRO MARTINEZ

Pitcher, Boston Red Sox
Height: 5' 11"   Weight: 170 pounds
Bats: Right   Throws: Right
Birth Date: October 25, 1971
Birth Place: Manoguayabo, Dominican Republic
Entered Majors: 1992

When Pedro Martinez pitches in Boston's Fenway Park, it's like a big party. Thousands of fans from his homeland of the Dominican Republic wave their country's flag. They sing songs and play musical instruments. And all the fans, whether they are from the Dominican Republic, the United States, or anywhere else, cheer *"Pe-dro! Pe-dro!"*

"I get really excited when I hear and see that," says Pedro. "It's a great feeling, how confident it makes you feel."

Pedro makes his teammates feel confident because he's such a good pitcher. Many people think he's the best in the game, and not just because he throws 95 miles per hour. He's outstanding because when he's on the mound, Pedro out-thinks the hitters.

"He's really smart," says first baseman Carlos Delgado of the Toronto Blue Jays. "He can read what you're looking for, a fastball, a curve, or a change-up. I don't know how he does it."

Says the Blue Jays' rightfielder Shawn Green: "It's fun to face him because it's a real challenge. You have to try to think what he's thinking. You can't afford to guess wrong. His fastball explodes on you."

Pedro won the National League Cy Young Award in 1997, when he pitched for the Montreal Expos. He had a 17–8 record and led the N.L. with a 1.90 earned run average (ERA). He won 19 games for the Red Sox in 1998, and passed the 20-win mark with the Sox in 1999.

Pedro has a great curveball. The power of his awesome fastball makes his change-up especially

Pedro is a fan favorite at Fenway.

FAST FACTS

☆ Struck out 10 or more batters in seven straight games in 1999

☆ Won the 1997 National League Cy Young Award while pitching for the Montreal Expos

☆ Struck out 305 batters in 1997

☆ Enjoys tossing packs of bubble gum to fans in stands before games

devastating. Batters expecting a full-speed fastball swing way too early for the slower change-up. Put those three pitches together, along with Pedro's smarts, and you have one of the game's great strikeout artists. In September 1999, he struck out 17 batters in one game — and that was against the world champion New York Yankees! At one point that season, Pedro had twice as many strikeouts as any other pitcher in the American League!

"Some days he just has nasty stuff," says Red Sox shortstop Nomar Garciaparra. "It should be illegal."

"He's so small, it's amazing he throws so fast." — Nomar Garciaparra, shortstop, Boston Red Sox

Pedro is amazingly focused on the mound. "He's so intense out there, his eyes are burning and everything," says Nomar. "It makes you want to go out there and try even harder behind him."

Being a hero to his fans in the Dominican Republic makes Pedro try harder, too. He donated money to build a church and a youth center in his homeland.

"My people need inspiration," says Pedro. "My people need role models. That's the main reason I try to behave myself and do things so well."

Pedro is one of the nicest guys in baseball — with some of the nastiest stuff!   ★

DAVID WELLS

Pitcher, Toronto Blue Jays
Height: 6' 4"   Weight: 225 pounds
Bats: Left   Throws: Left
Birth Date: May 20, 1963
Birth Place: Torrance,
California
Entered Majors: 1987

David Wells has been a New York Yankee fan all his life. After signing with the Bronx Bombers before the 1997 season, he said, "Now I can die happy."

But after two successful seasons in pinstripes, the Yankees traded David to the Toronto Blue Jays before the 1999 season. David was angry at first, but he didn't

Well, well, Wells. David is a top pitcher and a colorful character.

let it get him too down. He just packed his bags and became the best pitcher on the Blue Jays' staff! His arrival turned the Jays into playoff contenders. "I think the Yankees made a big mistake," says David. "I wanted to go out there and kick some butt."

David is nicknamed "Boomer" because of his weight, which often approaches 250 pounds. His personality is also big and booming. He has a reputation for doing and saying just about anything. He also has a lot of tattoos. One is of his son, Brandon, who was age 5 when David got the tattoo in 1997. Over the years, the tattoo is looking less and less like Brandon. "No problem," says David. "Someday I'll just have a mustache carved in."

> **"He always paints the corners with his pitches. Nothing's ever down the middle with David."**
> **— David Justice, leftfielder, Cleveland Indians**

David's hero is Babe Ruth, the legendary Yankee star. When David signed with the Yankees as a free agent, he wanted to wear uniform number 3, in honor of Babe. The team told him he couldn't because that number had been retired. So David chose number 33, instead. "This way, I can be the Babe twice over," he said.

David has spent more than $35,000 to buy Babe Ruth's jersey, bat, and hat and three baseballs signed by the slugger. One day in 1997, David wore the cap out to the mound at Yankee Stadium!

David once visited the Babe Ruth Museum, in Baltimore, Maryland. "The place gave me chills," says David. "I read the plaques on the walls. I checked out the memorabilia. I paced around the room he was born in. I went in feeling good and came out feeling great."

David's greatest moment came as a Yankee in 1998. He pitched a perfect game against the Minnesota Twins. In a perfect game, the pitcher retires all 27 opposing batters without giving up a hit or a walk. David was just the 13th major league pitcher to toss a perfect game. He proved that as funny as he is sometimes, he's a serious and dangerous pitcher when he's on the mound. He's especially dangerous in important games. David has won eight games and lost only one in the playoffs and World Series.

Opponents know what he can do. "He's coming after you," says his former Yankee teammate Paul O'Neill. "He has three or four different pitches, and they're all good. You better be ready to face him or he'll get you."   ★

FAST FACTS

☆ Threw a perfect game for the New York Yankees against the Minnesota Twins in 1998
☆ Struck out 16 batters in one game in 1997
☆ Pumps himself up by blasting heavy-metal music in the clubhouse before every start

MARIANO RIVERA

Relief Pitcher, New York Yankees
Height: 6' 2" **Weight: 170 pounds**
Bats: Right **Throws: Right**
Birth Date: November 29, 1969
Birth Place: Panama
City, Panama
Entered Majors: 1995

When Mariano Rivera is pitching for the New York Yankees, he looks calm and relaxed out on the mound. As he gets ready to throw the ball, he winds up slowly. Then, all of a sudden . . . *whoosh!* The pitch blows by the batter!

"The ball looks like it's coming out of a cannon," says outfielder David Justice

The Yankees like their chances with Mariano on the mound in the ninth.

of the Cleveland Indians. "Mariano's the nastiest closer in the game. He's awesome."

Mariano became the Yankees' closer in 1997. He saved 43 games with a tiny 1.88 earned run average (ERA). In 1998, he had 36 saves and a 1.91 ERA. He didn't miss a beat in 1999, succeeding in 20 of his first 21 chances to save a game.

"It's great when he comes in, because 99 percent of the time, it means we're going to win," says Yankee outfielder Paul O'Neill.

Mariano grew up in the Central American country of Panama. His family was too poor to buy proper baseball equipment. He sometimes had to make his own "baseballs" out of cardboard and tape. But Mariano worked hard to make it to the major leagues. There he helped the Yankees win the 1996 and 1998 World Series by blowing fastballs past the best hitters in the game.

One of those hitters is five-time All-Star Frank Thomas of the Chicago White Sox, also known as The Big Hurt. "You know his fastball is coming, and it's still tough to get a good swing on it."

The Big Hurt knows: Mariano means Big Trouble for his opponents. ★

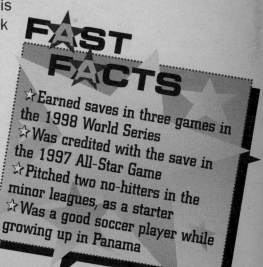

FAST FACTS

☆ Earned saves in three games in the 1998 World Series
☆ Was credited with the save in the 1997 All-Star Game
☆ Pitched two no-hitters in the minor leagues, as a starter
☆ Was a good soccer player while growing up in Panama

IVAN RODRIGUEZ

Catcher, Texas Rangers
Height: 5' 9"   **Weight: 205 pounds**
Bats: Right   **Throws: Right**
Birth Date: November 30, 1971
Birth Place: Vega Baja, Puerto Rico
Entered Majors: 1991

You can call it a gun or a cannon or a missile launcher. Whatever you call Ivan Rodriguez's throwing arm, make sure you call it the *best* in the major leagues.

"You just can't steal bases against him much," says speedster Bernie Williams of the New York Yankees. "He'll nail you."

Through 1998, Ivan had thrown out 46 percent of the runners who tried to steal on him in his major league career. His percentage of 53 in 1998 easily led the American League. Ivan's presense behind the plate keeps most baserunners glued to their bases.

Ivan is also great at blocking wild pitches and getting the most out of his pitching staff. He is definitely the best defensive catcher in baseball today. In fact, he may be the best defensive catcher ever!

"I think I have respect around the league for the things that I've done," says Ivan, who is also known by the nickname Pudge. "But I'm not done. I'm going to keep working hard and trying to get better every day."

It's hard to imagine Ivan getting better — behind the plate or *at* the plate. Ivan is one of the A.L.'s best hitters, too! In 1996, he hit 47 doubles, the most ever by a major league catcher. Ivan hit .300 or better every season from 1995 to 1998.

"He just hits line drives all over the place," says slugger Carlos Delgado of the Toronto Blue Jays. "He is a hitting machine."

Ivan played a lot of baseball while

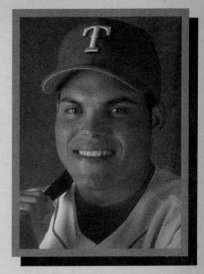

Ivan's awesome arm is the ultimate weapon against base-stealers.

FAST FACTS

☆ Won seven straight Gold Glove awards (1992 to 1998)

☆ In 1999, became the first catcher to hit 20 homers and steal 20 bases in the same season

☆ Loves watching drag racing and wants to try the sport someday

growing up in Puerto Rico. "We have good weather all year and play baseball all year long," he says. One of his Little League teammates was Juan Gonzalez, the Rangers' slugging outfielder. Juan and Ivan have been teammates with the Rangers for their entire careers!

When he was a kid, Ivan looked up to Johnny Bench, the Hall of Fame catcher for the Cincinnati Reds. "I liked to sit and watch the TV and pick up things about catching from him," says Ivan. "Then I would try to do those things on Saturday, when I played."

> "It's really tough to run on Ivan. He's got a great arm. He's the best I've ever played against."
> — Kenny Lofton, centerfielder, Cleveland Indians

Ivan learned fast. He reached the majors when he was just 19 years old! In his first big-league season, he caught for pitcher Nolan Ryan. Nolan was elected to the Baseball Hall of Fame in 1999. Now it looks as if Ivan is on the road to the Hall of Fame himself!

"Every year, Pudge has gotten better," says first baseman Will Clark of the Baltimore Orioles. "His arm strength gets better every year. His offense gets better. That's what makes him an all-star." ★

MO VAUGHN

First Baseman, Anaheim Angels
Height: 6' 1"   Weight: 245 pounds
Bats: Left   Throws: Right
Birth Date: December 15, 1967
Birth Place: Norwalk,
Connecticut
Entered Majors: 1991

At bat, Mo Vaughn looks like a really mean guy. The Anaheim Angel slugger is 245 pounds of pure muscle, and when he stands at the plate, he scowls at the pitcher. He looks as if he were going to bash every pitch to smithereens. When you get to know him, though, Mo is a very nice guy.

"I love to hang out and

Mo's powerful bat gives the Angel offense plenty of MOmentum.

17

have fun — laugh and joke around," says the first baseman.

Mo's teammates like to have fun with him, too. Once, they put a rubber snake in his locker. "I just ran," says Mo. "They knew I hated snakes, and they did it anyway!"

FAST FACTS

☆ Won the 1995 American League MVP award

☆ Hit .300 or better for the season five times through 1998

☆ Hit three home runs in one game twice (1996 and 1997)

☆ Nicknames include "Hit Dog" and "Big Mo"

Pitchers are even more afraid of Mo than he is of snakes. He's one of the scariest hitters in baseball. He hit .300 or more every season from 1994 through 1998, and he drove in at least 100 runs four times. Most of all, opponents know he can deliver. "When the game's on the line, you don't want to see big Mo up there," says New York Yankee pitcher David Cone.

Mo starred for the Boston Red Sox from 1991 through 1998. Mo grew up only a few hours from Boston, in Norwalk, Connecticut. Growing up, he had visited the city. His Aunt Loretta lived in Boston, and his family drove up there every year for Thanksgiving dinner. After Mo reached the major leagues, in 1991, he quickly became a team leader and one of Boston's most popular athletes.

But when Mo became a free agent, after the 1998 season, things changed. He and the Red Sox could not agree on a new contract. Mo chose to leave town — and head all the way across the country to Anaheim, California! The Angels and their fans were so happy that the team made up T-shirts that carried the slogan "The Beginning of the New Mollennium!" Mo printed T-shirts of his own for his new Angels teammates. They read "Together we can fly."

Mo bought a house on the Pacific Ocean, even though he doesn't take advantage of being on the beach. "I don't like going in the water — it has sharks and stuff." (And sea snakes!)

Mo's mother, Shirley, decorated his new house. Mo may be all grown up but he is still close to his parents. His father, Leroy, was a high school principal and youth-league baseball coach. "My father was very tough," says Mo. "But he's probably the friendliest man you'll ever meet."

Like father, like son.   ★

"Mo's a warrior. There probably isn't a better guy around to have on your team."
— Jeff Bagwell, first baseman, Houston Astros

ROBERTO ALOMAR

Second Baseman, Cleveland Indians
Height: 6'   **Weight: 185 pounds**
Bats: Switch-hitter   **Throws: Right**
Birth Date: February 5, 1968
Birth Place: Ponce, Puerto Rico
Entered Majors: 1988

Cleveland Indian second baseman Roberto Alomar has blazing speed, a quick bat, and soft hands for fielding ground balls. But it is Roberto's intelligence that sets him apart as the best all-around second baseman of the 1990's.

Roberto has a lot of baseball information stored inside his head. He always knows a lot about the starting pitcher he is facing on a particular day. That knowledge has helped Roberto hit better than .300 during his career. On defense, he knows where batters usually hit the ball so that he can be in the right spot to make the plays.

"Roberto is one of the smartest players in the game right now," says Indian shortstop Omar Vizquel. "He knows so much about everything."

Roberto learned a lot by growing up in a baseball family. His father, Sandy, played second base in the major leagues for 15 years. Roberto's older brother, Sandy, Junior, is the Indians' catcher.

The two brothers are very close, but the 1999 season was the first time they played a whole season on the same team. (Roberto had played for the San Diego Padres, Toronto Blue Jays, and Baltimore Orioles.)

Roberto and Sandy, Junior, had faced each other in the playoffs in 1996 and 1997, when Roberto played for the Orioles. They found it difficult to try to beat each other. They are much happier wearing the same uniform.

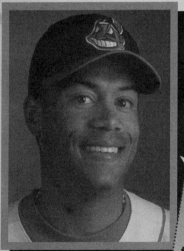

"It has been our dream to play in the big leagues together," says Roberto. "Now our dream has come true. This is the most fun I've ever had in baseball." ★

Roberto: Cleveland fans love his glove.

FAST FACTS

☆ Won seven Gold Glove awards in eight seasons, from 1991 to 1998
☆ Hit homers from both sides of the plate in one game four times (through 1998)
☆ Roberto and Sandy, Junior, are the only brothers to both be named All-Star Game MVP

TRAVIS FRYMAN

Third Baseman, Cleveland Indians
Height: 6' 4" **Weight: 195 pounds**
Bats: Right **Throws: Right**
Birth Date: March 25, 1969
Birth Place: Lexington, Kentucky
Entered Majors: 1990

You could call Cleveland Indian third baseman Travis Fryman Mr. Reliability. Year in and year out, the Cleveland Indians know what they're going to get from him: a hard-hitting bat and good defense. They also know that they can count on Travis to be in the lineup every day. When Travis went on the disabled list in 1999, it was

Travis went from thinking about quitting to thinking about hitting!

the first time he had been there in his nine-year career.

"I just want to play every day," says Travis. "If you play every day, you're going to put up a lot of numbers over time."

Travis has put up numbers. With the Detroit Tigers from 1991 through 1997, he hit between 15 and 22 home runs every year. In 1998, his first season with the Indians, he hit 28 homers, with 96 RBIs and a .287 batting average.

FAST FACTS

☆ Played in four All-Star Games (1992, 1993, 1994, 1996)
☆ Had 100 RBIs two straight years (1996, 1997)
☆ Led American League third basemen with a .978 fielding percentage in 1997
☆ Is an avid bow hunter

Success did not come easy for Travis. Early in his career, he struggled. Travis had a .234 batting average and only two home runs in his first two minor league seasons. He remembers sitting in his hotel room, thinking about quitting.

"But I decided to give baseball everything I had," says Travis. "You have to go through some down times so that you can appreciate when things are going well."

These days, things are going just fine for Mr. Reliability. ★

ALEX RODRIGUEZ

Shortstop, Seattle Mariners
Height: 6' 3"   Weight: 195 pounds
Bats: Right   Throws: Right
Birth Date: July 27, 1975
Birth Place: New York, New York
Entered Majors: 1994

Ask major league players about Alex Rodriguez, the Seattle Mariners' All-Star shortstop, and it sounds as if they're talking about one of the wonders of the world. "Alex can hit the ball as far as anyone in the game," says slugger Ron Coomer of the Minnesota Twins. Adds fellow Seattle slugger Edgar Martinez: "Alex has become a great player in a short time. He can hit, run, throw, and field the ball amazingly well."

Alex, nicknamed A-Rod, can do just about anything there is to do on the baseball field. On offense, he has the power to smash home runs and the speed to steal bases. On defense, Alex has the reflexes to field anything hit his way and the quickness to turn tough grounders into double plays. "He's just the total package," says Jay Bell of the Arizona Diamondbacks.

Alex didn't take long to prove he's one of the best — if not *the* best — players in the game. Alex turned 21 years old during the 1996 season. He celebrated with a season-long offensive explosion. Alex led the major leagues with a .358 batting average, blasted 36 home runs, and finished a close second in the American League MVP race.

"I think it was a surprise for everyone," Alex says of his breakout season. "It certainly was a pleasant surprise for me." A pleasant surprise that stands as one of the best seasons by a shortstop in baseball history.

Alex had some injuries in 1997 but still put up strong numbers. He finished with a .300 average and 84 runs batted in (RBIs). He also hit for the cycle, which means that he hit a single, a double, a triple, and a home run all in the same game!

A-Rod gets an "A" for effort *and* for results!

Alex's performance in 1997 set the stage for another awesome season in 1998. He hit .310, crushed 42 home runs, stole 46 bases, scored 123 runs, and drove in 124 more!

Those 42 home runs were the most ever in a season for a shortstop. And they made some fans wonder (see if you can believe this) whether Alex could become the next Mark McGwire.

"I think that Alex has a chance to break the home-run record," says Omar Vizquel, the star shortstop for the Cleveland Indians.

Alex can't compete against Big Mac in the power department just yet. But he does have a friendly rivalry with his good buddy Derek Jeter, the shortstop for the New York Yankees. "We enjoy competing against each other," says Derek. "When he hits a home run, he'll go sit on the bench and flex his arms at me."

Alex is friends with another baseball superstar, Cal Ripken, Junior, of the Baltimore Orioles. Cal was Alex's hero while Alex was growing up in Miami, Florida. Alex had a life-sized poster of Cal on the wall of his room. A few years ago, Alex got to play basketball against his childhood hero in the gym at Cal's house! "He dunked a few times, but not on me," says Cal. "I fouled him before I let him dunk on me."

FAST FACTS

☆ Hit 42 home runs and stole 46 bases in 1998 to become the first infielder in big-league history to join the "40-40 Club"

☆ Became Seattle's starting short-stop at just 18, in 1994

☆ Likes to read and is a big fan of William Shakespeare

Alex had one of the first bad breaks of his career in 1999 when he missed five weeks with a knee injury. People were worried that a bad leg would hamper him at the plate and in the field. But Alex wasn't all that worried.

"I got so many supportive letters from fans," says Alex. "People said that they had had the same surgery and that I would be back in action in no time. Reading all of those letters was very encouraging to me."

Sure enough, when he returned, Alex was as good as new. He hit two home runs in a game four times during the first half of the 1999 season. In June, he hit a 437-foot shot against the San Diego Padres. A-Rod's slugging stroke was back!

Despite his eye-popping statistics, Alex sets simple goals for himself. "I try to improve and to be consistent," he says. "If you're consistent, the numbers will be there to help the team win."

The unbelievable part is that Alex is still so young. His best performances could still be ahead of him. "I can't wait till I hit my prime," he says.

Watch out, Big Mac!   ★

"Alex has a very good chance to become the best shortstop ever."
— Cal Ripken, Junior, shortstop, Baltimore Orioles

KEN GRIFFEY, JUNIOR

Outfielder, Seattle Mariners
Height: 6' 3"   **Weight: 205 pounds**
Bats: Left   **Throws: Left**
Birth Date: November 21, 1969
Birth Place: Donora, Pennsylvania
Entered Majors: 1989

During the Great Home Run Race of 1998, Mark McGwire and Sammy Sosa grabbed all of the home-run headlines. Lost in all the fuss was the fact that centerfielder Ken Griffey, Junior, of the Seattle Mariners hit 56 home runs for the second straight season!

Junior led the American League in homers for the third time in his career. At 29 years of age, he became the youngest player ever to reach 350 career round-trippers.

Ken is so good that even his opponents are fans. Shawn Green of the Toronto Blue Jays grew up near Anaheim,

California. When the Mariners came to town to play the Angels, Shawn went to the games just to watch Junior play. And things haven't changed, now that Shawn has made it to the big leagues himself. "I'd still pay to see him play," says Shawn. "He's got such a pretty swing, and he just flies around the bases. He's just real fun to watch."

"When he comes up on TV, I'm definitely not switching the channel," agrees slugger Darin Erstad of the Angels.

Ken has always had a ton of talent. When he graduated from Moeller High School, in Cincin-, natti Ohio, in 1987, the Mariners picked him with the first pick in the amateur draft. One of the team's scouts said he had "superstar potential." Boy, was he right!

"I heard the

Complete player: Junior is as awesome in centerfield as he is at the plate.

FAST FACTS

☆ Won 1997 American League Most Valuable Player award
☆ Hit home runs in eight straight games in 1993, tying the major league record
☆ Loves playing video games. "I'm the unquestioned video-game king of the clubhouse," he says.

rumors about how good Junior was," says manager Joe Torre of the New York Yankees. Adds Joe, "All those rumors were true." Ken didn't take too long to prove that. He zoomed up the Mariners' minor league system and made it to the major leagues less than two years after he graduated from high school.

In 1990, one of Junior's teammates on the Mariners was his father, Ken Griffey, Senior. Senior was ending his own successful major league career. No father and son pair had ever played together in the major leagues.

"If you're a baseball fan, you have to be a fan of Ken Griffey, Junior. It seems like every day he's hitting another long home run."
— Mike Piazza, catcher, New York Mets

On September 14, 1990, the two Griffeys hit back-to-back home runs. They were the first father-son duo to accomplish that feat! "That was a dream come true," says Junior.

Junior is more than just a talented individual. He is also a great team player. Junior goes all out while patrolling center-field for Seattle. He dives, runs into outfield walls, and does whatever else it takes to make the catch. Junior led the Mariners to their first-ever playoff appearance in 1995. (They lost to the Cleveland Indians in the A.L. Championship Series.)

Despite his amazing statistics, Junior has never played in a World Series. A lot of fans talk about how he might break Hank Aaron's record of 755 career home runs some-day, but Junior has another goal. "I want to win a World

Series," he says. "I don't worry about home runs."

He isn't kidding. "I'm not trying to hit the ball 700 miles," says Junior. "I'm just trying to go up to the plate, swing the bat, and feel comfortable."

Junior makes it sound easy, doesn't he? But don't be fooled. He wouldn't have won an A.L. MVP award and nine straight Gold Gloves if he hadn't been a hard worker.

"He's worked hard for everything he's got," says Paul O'Neill of the New York Yankees. "He's accomplishing things that may never be accomplished again."

Junior has been so good for so long that people are running out of ways to praise him. Even his manager, Lou Piniella, has a hard time. "After you say he's the best in baseball, where do you go?" says Lou. "Junior is Junior, and there is no one else like him." ★

JUAN GONZALEZ

Outfielder, Texas Rangers
Height: 6' 3"   Weight: 220 pounds
Bats: Right   Throws: Right
Birth Date: October 16, 1969
Birth Place: Vega Baja,
Puerto Rico
Entered Majors: 1989

At 6-foot-3 and 220 pounds, outfielder Juan Gonzalez of the Texas Rangers seems to be made of muscles. But he didn't always look that way.

Juan grew up as a skinny kid in Vega Baja, Puerto Rico. In 1986, at the age of 16, he left his hometown to play minor league baseball for the Texas Rangers. He weighed just 175 pounds. His body

Juan "Gone" Gonzalez makes baseballs disappear — right over the fence!

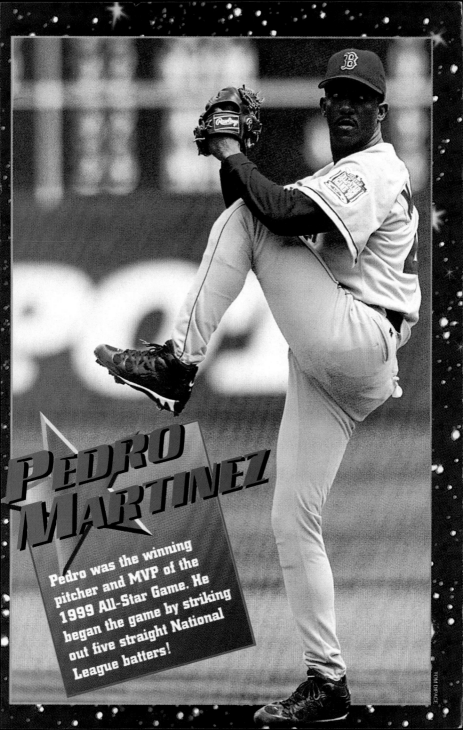

PEDRO MARTINEZ

Pedro was the winning pitcher and MVP of the 1999 All-Star Game. He began the game by striking out five straight National League batters!

TOM DIPACE

MIKE PIAZZA

Mike was named to the National League All-Star team in each of his first seven major league seasons. His .362 batting average for the Los Angeles Dodgers in 1997 was the highest ever by a catcher.

TOM DIPACE (2)

On August 5, 1999, Mark blasted his 500th career home run, against the San Diego Padres. He became the 16th major league player in history to hit 500 career home runs. He hit his 501st career home run later in the same game.

MARK McGWIRE

ROBERTO ALOMAR

Roberto played in every All-Star Game in the 1990's. He was named MVP of the 1998 All-Star Game. He had two singles and a home run to lead the American League to a 13–8 win.

PAUL JASIENSKI

CHIPPER JONES

Chipper is one of the best switch-hitters in the major leagues. He had at least 20 homers for four straight seasons from 1996-1999.

RON VESELY/MLB PHOTOS

ALEX RODRIGUEZ

Alex won the 1996 American League batting title with a .358 average. It was the highest average by a right-handed hitter since Joe DiMaggio hit .381 in 1939! In 1998, Alex hit 42 home runs. It was the most homers ever hit by an American League shortstop.

RON VESELY

MANNY RAMIREZ

Manny's powerful bat drives in loads of runs for the Cleveland Indians. In 1999, he had 96 RBIs *before* the All-Star Game. Only Hank Greenberg (103 RBIs in 1935) and Juan Gonzalez (101 RBIs in 1998) had ever driven in more runs during the first half of a major league season.

TOM DIPACE

SAMMY SOSA

In June 1998, Sammy had the best homer-hitting month in the history of major league baseball. He started the month with two home runs on June 1. He set the record when he hit his 20th homer of the month on June 30.

RON VESELY

KEN GRIFFEY, JUNIOR

Junior had 56 homers in 1998. He joined Babe Ruth and Mark McGwire as the only players to hit at least 50 homers two seasons in a row. He also became the youngest player to hit 350 career home runs.

was all arms and legs.

Juan did not hit any home runs in his first season in the minors. He also struck out a lot. But the people who saw him play could tell that he had tons of potential. One of his teammates, current Chicago Cub slugger Sammy Sosa, believed Juan would explode someday.

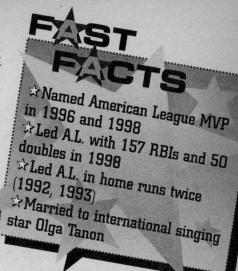

FAST FACTS

☆ Named American League MVP in 1996 and 1998
☆ Led A.L. with 157 RBIs and 50 doubles in 1998
☆ Led A.L. in home runs twice (1992, 1993)
☆ Married to international singing star Olga Tanon

"He was a player who had the talent and the ability," says Sammy. "At first, he didn't hit so many home runs. Then he started working out every day, doing what he was supposed to be doing, then, BOOM!"

Boom is right. Juan got bigger and stronger. He hit 14 home runs the next season. In 1989, he reached the majors for good. Since then Juan has established himself as one of baseball's top sluggers. He hit a career-high 47 homers in 1996. In 1998, he smashed his 300th career home run.

Juan's best skill is driving in runs. In 1998, he led the American League with 157 runs batted in. It was the most in the A.L. since 1949, when Vern Stephens and Ted Williams each had 159 RBIs for the Boston Red Sox.

When there are men on base and Juan needs a clutch hit, he doesn't swing for the fences. He tries to get a single or a double to drive in a run and keep the rally going.

"When I see men on base, I'm trying hard," says Juan. "I have more concentration and I'm more patient. I'm focusing on driving those runners in."

It's amazing that the skinny kid has grown up to be one of the game's most fearsome hitters. It's also amazing that Juan and Sammy Sosa were once on the same minor league team. That team must have had a great lineup!

The Rangers traded Sammy to the Chicago White Sox in 1989, so the two never played on the same team in the major leagues. But they have both become big stars. In 1998, they each were named Most Valuable Player. It was Juan's second MVP award.

"You never want to see Juan coming up to the plate. You make a mistake, and he'll hit it a long, long way." — David Cone, pitcher, New York Yankees

"We had the same dreams, Sammy and I," Juan remembers. Now those dreams have come true.   ★

MANNY RAMIREZ

Outfielder, Cleveland Indians
Height: 6'   Weight: 205 pounds
Bats: Right   Throws: Right
Birth Date: May 30, 1972
Birth Place: Santo
Domingo, Dominican
Republic
Entered Majors: 1993

First baseman Jim Thome of the Cleveland Indians is really glad he's not a pitcher. "I'd be scared to face Manny Ramirez," says Jim. "Look at his numbers!"

Okay, let's do that. The Indians' slugging rightfielder hit 45 home runs in 1998. He was also one of the best RBI men in the major leagues,

Manny is the main man in Cleveland!

driving in 145 runs. "Every time we need a run, he finds a way to bring it home," says Indian shortstop Omar Vizquel. "I just hope he doesn't get tired."

Manny put up his best numbers ever in the first half of the 1999 season. He had 96 RBIs at the All-Star break. In September, he broke the club record of 162 RBIs set by Hal Trosky in 1936. Only eight men in *major league history* have driven in more runs in a season than Manny, who had 165 RBIs. He also batted a whopping .333!

Manny is six feet tall. That's not huge by big-league standards. But he's extremely strong and has great hand-to-eye coordination. He always seems to hit the ball *hard.*

"He has as much talent as anyone in the game right now," the Indians' manager Mike Hargrove said in 1999.

Although others believed in him, Manny didn't always believe in himself. He had been one of America's top high school sluggers while growing up in New York City. But he says he was scared when he was drafted by the Indians in 1991 and sent to one of their minor league teams.

FAST FACTS

☆Had more than 100 RBIs in one season four times through 1999
☆Hit home runs in four straight at-bats (1998)
☆Hit 13 career home runs in the post-season through 1999
☆Nicknamed the "Baby Bull" because of his strength

"I wondered, What if I don't make it?" says Manny. He spent hundreds of dollars on phone bills calling home from the minor leagues. "But I took my chances, and I just went out and tried my best."

His best was more than enough! Manny flew up the minor-league ladder. Within three years, he had become the Indians' starting rightfielder! He batted better than .300 every season from 1995 to 1997. Then he had those 145 RBIs in 1998 and became a full-fledged superstar in 1999.

One of the secrets of Manny's success is that he always keeps himself on an even keel. "Nothing bothers him. He isn't rattled by anything," says the Indians' leftfielder David Justice. "He'll strike out and act like it's nothing. He puts his bat back in the rack and gets his glove to go play defense. I would like to get inside Manny's head one day and see how he does it."

Manny insists that he has a very simple approach to batting: "Sometimes I get the pitcher, and sometimes the pitcher gets me."

> **"Manny plays to have fun. He enjoys the game, and doesn't put pressure on himself."**
> **— Mike Jackson, pitcher, Cleveland Indians**

Don't be modest, Manny. You get the best of pitchers more often than just about anyone these days! ★

JOSE CANSECO

Designated Hitter, Tampa Bay Devil Rays
Height: 6' 4"   **Weight: 240 pounds**
Bats: Right   **Throws: Right**
Birth Date: July 2, 1964
Birth Place: Havana, Cuba
Entered Majors: 1985

In the 1980s, when Jose Canseco and Mark McGwire both played for the Oakland Athletics, they were known as "the Bash Brothers" because of the tremendous home runs they both hit. Jose was full of "bash" — he hit 42 home runs in 1988 — but he was also full of flash. Back then, the burly slugger liked to get lots of attention. He had fancy red sports cars and hung out with Madonna. Jose acted as if he were the best baseball player in the world.

The truth is, he *was* among the world's best players. He had great power and surprising speed. In 1988, Jose became the first major leaguer ever to steal 40 bases and hit 40 home runs in the same season. Since then, only two players (Barry Bonds and Alex Rodriguez) have matched that feat.

After suffering many injuries in the 1990's, though, Jose has changed. The Tampa Bay Devil Ray designated hitter is still a home-run hitter. He slugged 31 homers in the first half of the 1999 season before being slowed by a back injury. But Jose has slowed down on the base paths, and he has also cooled his lifestyle.

"I just want to go about my business," says Jose.

Jose hit his 400th career home run early in 1999. He might have been at 500, or more, but injuries kept him out of hundreds of games in the 1990's. If he does hit 500 homers, he'll have a good chance to reach the Hall of Fame.

"I think it's still just a matter of time before I reach the 500 and 600 levels," says Jose. "With the ability I have, I think I can play until I'm 40 years old and beyond." ★

**Sneak a fastball
by this man?
No way, Jose!**

FAST FACTS

☆ Hit three home runs in one game twice (1988 and 1994)

☆ Became the first player to have at least 40 steals and 40 homers in one season, in 1988

☆ Won the 1986 American League Rookie of the Year award and the 1988 A.L. MVP award

National League Starting Lineup

RHP	Kevin Brown, Los Angeles Dodgers
LHP	Randy Johnson, Arizona Diamondbacks
RP	Trevor Hoffman, San Diego Padres
C	Mike Piazza, New York Mets
1B	Mark McGwire, St. Louis Cardinals
2B	Craig Biggio, Houston Astros
3B	Chipper Jones, Atlanta Braves
SS	Barry Larkin, Cincinnati Reds
OF	Sammy Sosa, Chicago Cubs
OF	Barry Bonds, San Francisco Giants
OF	Larry Walker, Colorado Rockies

KEVIN BROWN

Pitcher, Los Angeles Dodgers
Height: 6' 4" **Weight: 200 pounds**
Bats: Right **Throws: Right**
Birth Date: March 14, 1965
Birth Place: McIntyre, Georgia
Entered Majors: 1986

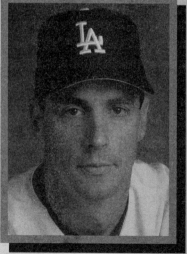

Batters don't need their eyes to figure out that Los Angeles Dodger ace Kevin Brown is pitching to them. They can use their ears. Kevin's fastball is so fast, and it spins so hard, that it makes a *sssssst!* sound as it crosses the plate. Kevin's fastball hisses like a snake, and it's just as nasty!

Kevin's awesome pitching

Bat-breaker: Leave your favorite bat at home when you face Kevin Brown!

41

skills have led two different teams to the World Series. He helped the Florida Marlins win the Series in 1997. A year later, he sparked the San Diego Padres to the Fall Classic. (They lost, in four games, to the New York Yankees.) Kevin's leadership is one of the main reasons the Dodgers gave him a huge $105 million contract before the start of the 1999 season.

FAST FACTS

☆ Pitched a 9-0 no-hitter over the San Francisco Giants, in 1997
☆ Helped the Florida Marlins win the 1997 World Series by posting a 16-8 record that season
☆ Loves the old TV show "Star Trek" and has 89 episodes of it in his video library

"Kevin's a winner," says Davey Johnson, the Dodgers' manager. "He gives you everything he's got."

From 1996 to 1998, Kevin had a 51–26 record with a puny 2.33 earned run average. His 97-mile-per-hour fastball is so hard that it splinters opponents' bats right in their hands! When Kevin was playing for the Texas Rangers, teammates called him "Chain Saw," because his pitches broke so many bats.

"You might be in a streak, using your favorite bat for two weeks, but odds are when you face Kevin, that bat's going to be in six pieces by the time the game's over," says Larry Walker, the rightfielder for the Colorado Rockies.

Kevin wasn't always such a devastating pitcher. He grew up in tiny McIntyre, Georgia. When he went to college at

Georgia Technical University, in 1983, he had no intention of playing on the baseball team. But after the coaches there saw him pitch one day, they asked him to play. "They brought me inside, gave me a locker, and said, 'Congratulations. You're on the team,' " says Kevin.

He has been a standout ever since, partly because of his attitude. "When I take the ball, I have one thing on my mind — winning," says Kevin. "I don't let anything distract me. I don't let anything stand in my way."

Kevin is known for being very tough, almost mean, on the mound. He stares down hitters and isn't afraid to "brush them back" by pitching the ball to the inside part of home plate. Sometimes he pitches too far inside. He has twice led his league in hitting batters. Needless to say, most hitters don't exactly look forward to facing him. But Rockies slugger Larry Walker says he doesn't mind trying to hit Kevin all that much.

> "He throws really hard, 96 or 97 miles an hour. And he doesn't throw the ball straight like other guys. His ball really moves and sinks."
> — Matt Williams, third baseman, Arizona Diamondbacks

"It's kind of a privilege and an honor to face Kevin," says Larry, "because he's so good."

Yeah, right, tell that to your poor bat!   ★

RANDY JOHNSON

Pitcher, Arizona Diamondbacks
Height: 6' 10"   Weight: 230 pounds
Bats: Right   Throws: Left
Birth Date: September 10, 1963
Birth Place: Walnut Creek, California
Entered Majors: 1988

When hitters walk up to the plate to hit against Randy Johnson's 98-mile-per-hour fastballs, they have to turn their brains off.

"You can't think when a guy's pitching that fast," says Baltimore Oriole slugger Will Clark. "You have to do all your thinking in the on-deck circle. Once you're at bat, you barely have enough time just to react."

Randy is the Arizona Diamondbacks' ace pitcher. He is one of the greatest strikeout pitchers in the history of the major leagues. He's the only starting pitcher ever to average more than 10 strikeouts per nine innings in his career. That's even better than all-time strikeout king Nolan Ryan!

Would you believe that Randy doesn't concentrate on

throwing as hard as he can? "It's the times when I'm out there and relaxed that I throw my best and my hardest," he says.

He believes that throwing hard isn't as important as throwing strikes. "I've been clocked at 100 miles an hour, but I'd rather throw 95 and be able to hit the corners of the strike zone," he says. "No matter how hard you throw, major league hitters can hit a ball that's right down the middle."

It took Randy many years to learn how to throw the ball over the plate. At 6' 10", he is the tallest player in major league history. He had a hard time controlling his long arms and legs to get the ball to go exactly where he wanted it to go. Sometimes, when he was in the minor leagues in the mid-1980's, his wild pitches flew over the backstop!

In 1989, Randy made it to the major leagues with the Seattle Mariners. But he still needed to work hard on his

Nearly seven feet tall, "The Big Unit" is big trouble for batters.

FAST FACTS

☆ Struck out 300 or more batters in one season three times (1993, 1998, 1999)

☆ In 1990, pitched a no-hitter for the Seattle Mariners against the Detroit Tigers

☆ Likes to play the drums and shoot photography

control. He sometimes lost games because he walked so many batters. He led the league in walks three times. In 1990, Randy threw a no-hitter for the Mariners against the Detroit Tigers. The first question his father asked him afterward was, "How many walks did you have?" (Randy walked six.)

In 1992, Randy learned some control pointers from — who else? — Nolan Ryan, who was then pitching for the Texas Rangers. Ever since then, Randy has been rolling. From 1995 through 1998, he won 62 games and lost just 17! He has led his league in strikeouts five times. More important, he has not led his league in *walks* since 1992.

> **"It isn't fun to face him, but it's a challenge. You have to work incredibly hard."**
> **— Tony Gwynn, rightfielder, San Diego Padres**

Randy's height no longer is a problem for him on the mound. Instead, it now is an advantage, because it intimidates hitters. "It's almost like he's touching you in the nose when he releases the ball," says rightfielder Brian Jordan of the Atlanta Braves. "He's tough!"

One of the toughest ever. ★

TREVOR HOFFMAN

Relief Pitcher, San Diego Padres
Height: 6' **Weight: 205 pounds**
Bats: Right **Throws: Right**
Birth Date: October 13, 1967
Birth Place: Bellflower,
California
Entered Majors: 1993

Trevor Hoffman of the San Diego Padres is the best closer in the National League. He enters the game in the ninth inning and shuts the door on the opposition.

But Trevor doesn't just sit in the Padres' bullpen waiting until it's time for him to come into the game. Would you believe that instead of hanging out where most

It's all over for the Padres' opponents when Trevor enters the game.

47

relief pitchers do, he takes a shower and watches TV?

Yep, in the fifth or sixth inning, Trevor goes to the club-house shower and runs warm water over his arm to loosen it up. "Then I stretch in front of the TV and watch at-bats of players from that game," says Trevor. "I want to have a bet-ter idea of what to do when I go into a ball game."

When Trevor walks out to pitch the ninth inning in San Diego, the Qualcomm Stadium speakers blast heavy metal music to get Trevor and the fans pumped up. "My goal is to get three outs, not to bring my guitar out there and do a solo," says Trevor. "But it's fun."

Batters don't think it's much fun to face Trevor. He tied the N.L. record for saves in one season by saving 53 games in 1998. Trevor's reliable success in the ninth inning helped lead the Padres to the World Series.

Not bad — especially for a guy who was a poor-hitting shortstop in the minor leagues before he decided he wanted to give pitching a try in 1991!

"I had a pretty good arm, so I decided, Why not give it a shot on the hill?" says Trevor.

Trevor's shot turned out to be a bull's-eye! ★

FAST FACTS

☆ Tied the National League record for saves in one season with 53, in 1998

☆ One of his older brothers, Glenn, was a major league infielder from 1980 to 1989 and managed the Los Angeles Dodgers in 1998

☆ Loves to surf in the off-season

MIKE PIAZZA

Catcher, New York Mets

Height: 6' 3" **Weight: 215 pounds**

Bats: Right **Throws: Right**

Birth Date: September 4, 1968

Birth Place: Norristown, Pennsylvania

Entered Majors: 1992

Catcher Mike Piazza is so strong even the scoreboard begs for mercy! The New York Mets' slugger was taking batting practice one day at Shea Stadium. He blasted two balls off the centerfield scoreboard and smashed light bulbs. A few minutes later, the scoreboard flashed the message: "Mike, Please Don't Hurt Me!"

Catch this: Mike has tons of power at the plate.

49

Mike has put the hurt on a lot of opponents since he reached the major leagues in 1992. He hits around .330 every year and has averaged 33 home runs per season.

"He's a guy you really want to stay away from," says ace pitcher Randy Johnson of the Arizona Diamondbacks. "He can hit the ball to all fields — and a long way if he really gets a hold of it."

Mike didn't always get that kind of respect for his base-ball skills. He didn't even get drafted when he graduated from high school in 1986! Two years later, he *did* get draft-ed by the Los Angeles Dodgers, largely because his father, Vince, was friends with Tommy Lasorda. Tommy was the Dodgers' manager at the time. Still, Mike wasn't drafted until the 62nd round!

Mike had to fight his way up the minor league ladder to make it to the majors. When times get hard for him today, Mike reminds himself of how far he has come since high school. He remembers how hard he worked and how he refused to give up.

"Nothing good ever comes easy," says Mike. "Once I put my mind to something, I give it 100 per-cent of my effort."

Mike enjoys tel-ling his inspira-tional story to kids. He has spoken to lots of schools and

FAST FACTS

☆ Won the 1993 N.L. Rookie of the Year award with the Los Angeles Dodgers

☆ Played in the All-Star Game in each of his first seven full seasons

☆ Is a big heavy-metal music fan, and enjoys banging on his drum set to relax

youth groups about how to persevere during tough times.

"I always try to explain that you should never give up when you put your mind to something," says Mike. "You always have fear of something — fear of failure, fear of letting yourself down. But you have to put that out of your mind."

Mike likes filling his mind with information about baseball's past. He reads lots of books on baseball history and looks up statistics on the game's legends.

"Being a player, I can talk to a lot of people and ask, 'Hey, what kind of player was [former All-Star third baseman] Mike Schmidt? Or [Hall of Fame catcher] Johnny Bench?' It's really cool," says Mike. "It's great. I not only play the game, but I'm also a big fan of the game and its history."

> "I like watching Mike play. He's got one of those booming bats. You never know how far the ball's going to go."
> — Ivan Rodriguez, catcher, Texas Rangers

The way he's hitting these days, Mike might just rewrite some of that history! ★

MARK McGWIRE

First Baseman, St. Louis Cardinals
Height: 6' 5"   **Weight: 250 pounds**
Bats: Right   **Throws: Right**
Birth Date: October 1, 1963
Birth Place: Pomona, California
Entered Majors: 1986

Unless you've lived on the moon for the last few years, you know that slugger Mark McGwire of the St. Louis Cardinals hit 70 home runs in 1998 to set a major league record. And if you have been living on the moon, then you might have seen at least one of his home runs land there! That's how far he seems to hit them!

But there's more to Mark than his great '98. There's more to him than baseball, even. Here's the ultimate list of interesting facts about Big Mac:

✳ Mark can hit a golf ball 350 yards, longer than many top pro golfers. When he was a sophomore in high school, Mark actually quit baseball to join the golf team. He returned to the diamond a year later. Thank goodness!

✳ Mark was mainly a pitcher in high school and at the beginning of his college career. He was good, too. In 1983, during his sophomore year at the University of Southern California (USC), he had a 2.78 earned run average. One of his fellow pitchers at USC was Randy Johnson, now an All-Star with the Arizona Diamondbacks.

✳ Mark hit the longest home run of his career in 1998, at Busch Stadium, in St. Louis, Missouri. His 545-foot bomb smashed into an advertising sign on the grandstand. To mark the spot, the team patched the sign with a giant Band-Aid!

✳ Mark has inspired lots of kids over the past few years, but his father, John, is an inspiration, too. John McGwire had polio when he was a boy. Because of the disease, John had to spend seven months in bed. When he recovered, he walked with a limp and had to wear a leg brace. But John still learned how to box and play golf, and he once rode his bicycle 300 miles!

✳ Mark was born on October 1, 1963. That's two years to the day after Roger Maris of the New York Yankees hit his 61st home run of the 1961 season. Roger's 61 in '61 set the major league record that Mark

Big Mac: Home-run hero Mark McGwire

shattered in 1998.

✳ Mark isn't the only athletic member of his family. His younger brother Dan was a backup quarterback for the Seattle Seahawks and the Miami Dolphins from 1991 to 1995. His other brothers played sports too.

✳ Mark has been putting on batting-practice displays since he was in college. He played for the 1984 U.S. Olympic team with many future major leaguers, including current Cincinnati Red shortstop Barry Larkin. Barry remembers Mark hitting 500-foot moon shots all over Dodger Stadium, in Los Angeles. "He was hitting bombs, almost out of the stadium," Barry says. When that Olympic team played in Fenway Park, in Boston, Hall of Fame slugger Reggie Jackson saw Mark slam one. "That's the longest ball I've ever seen hit," said Reggie.

✳ Mark is very nearsighted, which means he can see things clearly only when they are very close to him. He wears contact lenses and can see baseballs as they are pitched to him, but he often loses sight of his blasts before the ball reaches the outfield stands. Mark knows he has walloped a home run when he hears the crowd roar.

✳ The New York Mets wanted to select Mark with the

FAST FACTS

☆ Hit 70 home runs in 1998 to break a 37-year-old major league record for homers in one season
☆ Helped the Oakland A's reach the World Series in 1988, 1989, and 1990 (They won in 1989.)
☆ Mark's father, John, is a dentist, and Mark has never had a cavity

number 1 overall pick in the 1984 draft, but they weren't sure he would sign a contract with them. So they took another player instead — an outfielder from Pennsylvania named Shawn Abner. Shawn wound up hitting only 11 home runs in his major league career. *Oops!*

✳ Mark hit at least 50 homers in every season from 1996 to 1999. No other major leaguer had ever hit that many in four straight years. Mark had a chance to reach 50 as a rookie in 1987, too. He had 49 home runs but decided to skip the last game of the season and fly home. His wife at the time, Kathy, was about to give birth to their son, Matthew. Mark wanted to be there.

"I was thinking, 'I'll never have another first child,' " says Mark, " 'but I will have another chance to hit 50 home runs.' "

> "The rest of us aim for the front row of the seats. Mark aims for the back row."
> — Steve Finley, outfielder, Arizona Diamondbacks

Mark was right. And when he finally did hit his 50th homer in one season, in 1996, he gave the ball to Matt! ★

CRAIG BIGGIO

Second Baseman, Houston Astros
Height: 5' 11"   **Weight: 180 pounds**
Bats: Right   **Throws: Right**
Birth Date: December 14, 1965
Birth Place: Smithtown, New York
Entered Majors: 1988

Craig Biggio of the Houston Astros will do *anything* to help his team.

Craig began his big-league career as a catcher. In 1991, he made the All-Star team as a catcher. But then the Astros needed him to switch to second base. Craig learned his new position so well, he became an All-Star there, too!

"I spent a lot of years playing catcher, but I was able to make a smooth adjustment to second base," says Craig. "A big part of baseball is making adjustments."

When Craig is on top of his game, it's the other teams that have to adjust to him. He can win a game with his bat, his glove, or his legs. Craig batted .306 from 1995 to 1998 and averaged 20 home runs and 126 runs scored per year.

He also averaged 39 stolen bases. And he did it all while winning three Gold Glove awards as the best-fielding second baseman in the league.

"I take my defense as seriously as I take my hitting and my baserunning," says Craig. "I take the whole game seriously, not just certain parts of the game."

Although Craig has put up fancy individual statistics, he always stays focused on team goals. The Astros won the National League Central Division in 1997 and 1998. The 1997 title was the first one the team had won since Craig joined the club in 1988.

"When you work so hard for something and then you finally reach it," says Craig, "it is the greatest feeling in the world." ★

With his great all-around game, Craig is second to none at second base.

FAST FACTS

☆ Has hit over .300 four times through the 1998 season
☆ Won four straight Gold Gloves, from 1994 to 1997
☆ Donates time and money to the Sunshine Kids, a charity in Houston that helps children with cancer

CHIPPER JONES

Third Baseman, Atlanta Braves
Height: 6' 4"   **Weight: 210 pounds**
Bats: Both   **Throws: Right**
Birth Date: April 24, 1972
Birth Place: De Land, Florida
Entered Majors: 1993

Third baseman Chipper Jones of the Atlanta Braves is the best switch-hitter in the National League. He is dangerous from both sides of the plate. When it comes to hitting home runs, though, he's especially dangerous when he bats left-handed. In Chipper's first four full seasons in the major leagues, he smacked 108 homers.

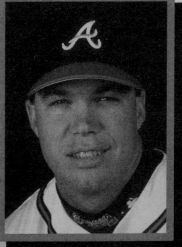

Fun fact: Chipper's real name is Larry Wayne Jones, Junior.

Ninety-six of those home runs came batting left-handed. So Chipper must be naturally left-handed, right? Wrong! He grew up hitting righty only!

Chipper learned to hit lefty in high school. His father, Larry, taught him in the Jones's backyard.

Chipper almost gave up switch-hitting in 1990, his first year in the minor leagues. "But I was told to stick with it," he says. "It started clicking in 1991. Balls started jumping out of the park. Look where switch-hitting has gotten me."

FAST FACTS

☆ Drove in more than 100 runs each season from 1996 to 1999
☆ Three-time All-Star
☆ Hit 23 home runs and had 86 runs batted in as a rookie in 1995. He also helped the Braves win the World Series that year.
☆ Loves hunting and fishing

Through 1999, Chipper's career batting average was over .300, and he had driven in more than 100 runs in every season from 1996 to 1999. His great hitting ability helped the Braves win two N.L. titles and the 1995 World Series.

"Chipper is one of the most consistent players around," says New York Met catcher Mike Piazza. "He's a gamer."

Switch-hitting is hard, but Chipper says anyone can try it. "Take 100 at-bats off a tee every day from your weak side. Do it for two weeks, till it becomes natural," he says. "Then get a buddy or a parent to go out and soft-toss to you."

If you want to make it to the majors like Chipper, this might be the right — or left — way to start. ★

BARRY LARKIN

Shortstop, Cincinnati Reds
Height: 6'   **Weight: 185 pounds**
Bats: Right   **Throws: Right**
Birth Date: April 28, 1964
Birth Place: Cincinnati, Ohio
Entered Majors: 1986

Few major leaguers can hit, run, and catch as well as Barry Larkin. After all, the Cincinnati Reds' shortstop is a 10-time All-Star and former National League MVP. But physical ability is only part of the story. Barry is also one of the smartest players in the game. He's always a step ahead of the other team. He knows what situations will come up during a game and how to react to them.

"Homers and huge plays make the highlights," says Barry. "But it's the little things that usually win baseball games. Those things come from out-thinking your opponents."

Here's an example: A few years ago, a Philadelphia Phillie base runner took a long lead off second base. Barry wanted to tell the Reds' second baseman, Mariano Duncan, to signal for a pickoff throw from the pitcher. So he just yelled it out to Mariano — in Spanish! — so the runner wouldn't understand.

The plan worked and the runner was picked off. Barry smiled from ear to ear, trying not to laugh. Barry had learned to speak Spanish while he was in the minor leagues, so that he could communicate better with Hispanic teammates. The lessons paid off.

"It's a great feeling to know you just completely outsmarted someone," says Barry. "A lot of times, an inch of advantage makes all the difference in baseball. Usually, that tiny break comes from being mentally prepared."

Smart words from a smart player.   ★

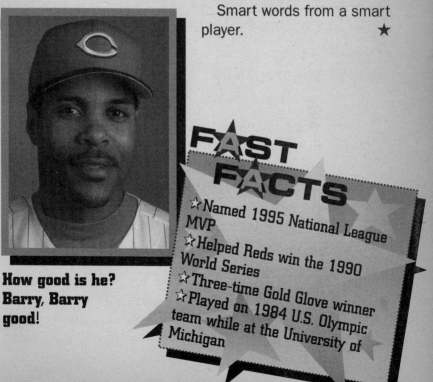

How good is he? Barry, Barry good!

FAST FACTS

☆ Named 1995 National League MVP
☆ Helped Reds win the 1990 World Series
☆ Three-time Gold Glove winner
☆ Played on 1984 U.S. Olympic team while at the University of Michigan

SAMMY SOSA

Rightfielder, Chicago Cubs
Height: 6'   **Weight: 210 pounds**
Bats: Right   **Throws: Right**
Birth Date: November 12, 1968
Birth Place: San Pedro de Macoris, Dominican Republic
Entered Majors: 1989

Sammy Sosa of the Chicago Cubs takes baseball very seriously. How else could he have hit more than 60 home runs in 1998 and 1999? But he also makes sure to have fun on the field. He often takes a playful hop when he sees one of his homers zoom out of the park. He also blows kisses to the fans at Wrigley Field, in Chicago.

And the fans love Sammy. They chant *"Sam-MEE! Sam-MEE!"* when he's at bat and when he runs out to rightfield at the start of the game. They have fun and he has fun. "I enjoy everything that I do," says Sammy. "I'm happy."

Even opponents notice how much fun Sammy has. "He gets fans on their feet. I think that's great," says John

Olerud, the first baseman for the New York Mets. "He is having fun, so they are having fun. He gets the fans into the game."

Times weren't always so much fun for Sammy. He grew up in San Pedro de Macoris, in the Dominican Republic. His father died when Sammy was 7, leaving behind a family that was already poor. Sammy shined shoes, washed cars, and sold oranges to earn money for his mother, four brothers, and two sisters.

Without much money, Sammy couldn't afford real baseball equipment as a kid. He used a milk carton for a glove and balled-up socks for baseballs. Sammy remembers those times now when he's struggling on the baseball field.

"I never feel pressure," he says. "Pressure was when I was a kid and didn't have any food on the table."

These days Sammy earns more than $10 million per year and has a good life. But he hasn't forgotten about people less fortunate than him back in the Dominican Republic. Sammy helped build a mall in his hometown. He bought 250 computers for schools and built a baseball school there for kids. When Hurricane Georges devastated the Dominican

Slammin' Sammy slugged 60-plus homers in both 1998 and 1999.

Republic, in 1998, Sammy raised money and delivered food to help the victims of the terrible storm.

For his charity work, Sammy received the 1998 Roberto Clemente Award. That was a big honor for Sammy. Roberto Clemente was a Hall of Fame outfielder for the Pittsburgh Pirates. He died in a plane crash in 1972 while delivering supplies to earthquake victims in Nicaragua. Roberto was one of Sammy's heroes. Sammy wears number 21 to honor Roberto, who wore that number.

Sammy wants to help other people as much as Roberto did. "I had a hard time when I was a kid. I never had the opportunity to enjoy a lot," says Sammy. "Now that I am what I am, I'm trying to give something back, something that I never had before."

Before 1998, Sammy never had really big success. He joined the major leagues in 1989, but had never hit more than 40 home runs in a season. Usually, he swung too hard and struck out too much.

"I was trying to hit two home runs in every at-bat," says Sammy. "I was trying to prove so much."

That changed in 1998. Sammy became a better hitter — and next thing he knew, he was in the midst of the Great Home-Run

FAST FACTS

☆ Won the National League MVP award in 1998 after he hit 66 home runs and led the major leagues with 158 RBIs
☆ Hit three home runs in a game twice (1996, 1998). The first time, he hit both homers in one inning!
☆ Likes to box and watch football

Race with Mark McGwire. Sammy hit 66 home runs, six more than Babe Ruth. He also had a .308 batting average and led the major leagues with 158 RBIs. He helped the Cubs to the playoffs and was named the N.L. MVP.

In 1999, Sammy proved that he was one of the best sluggers of all time when he became the first player to hit 60 home runs in a season twice. He finished 1999 with 63 homers and 141 RBIs. Mark McGwire joined the club later in the 1999 season.

No question Sammy delivers great statistics for the Cubs, but his teammates know that there's more to him than just big numbers. "Sammy isn't just a great hitter," says Mark Grace, the Cubs' first baseman. "He always plays with a smile. He's fun to be around."

Unless you're a pitcher for the other team! ★

"Sammy's amazing. He's not that big, but he has incredible power."
—Mike Piazza, catcher, New York Mets

BARRY BONDS

Outfielder, San Francisco Giants
Height: 6' 2"   Weight: 210 pounds
Bats: Left   Throws: Left
Birth Date: July 24, 1964
Birth Place: Riverside,
California
Entered Majors: 1986

Barry Bonds grew up surrounded by baseball. His father, Bobby, was a three-time major league All-Star. His godfather, Willie Mays, is a Hall of Fame outfielder who hit 660 home runs in his career. Bobby and Willie became good friends while playing the outfield together for the San Francisco Giants from 1968 to 1972. Young

Barry learned to play baseball from two major league masters.

Barry looked up to both of them.

"There wasn't any kid growing up in San Francisco who didn't want to be Willie Mays," says Barry, now a slugger for the Giants himself. "Willie was always challenging me. He inspired me and pushed me. I remember playing around with him in the locker room."

FAST FACTS

☆ Has won three National League MVP awards (1990, 1992, 1993)
☆ Played in eight All-Star Games
☆ First major leaguer to hit 400 home runs and steal 400 bases
☆ Has won eight Gold Gloves
☆ Loves to surf the internet and has several computers

Willie and Bobby were the first two major leaguers to hit 30 home runs and steal 30 bases in the same season two years in a row. Bobby learned to play baseball the same way, using his power to hurt opponents at the plate and his speed to hurt them on the bases. In 1998, Barry became the first major league player ever to hit more than 400 home runs and steal more than 400 bases in his career. Like Willie, Barry is also a great defensive player. Many people think he might be the best fielding leftfielder of all time.

"Barry can beat you any way possible," says Art Howe, the manager of the Oakland Athletics. "Usually, when you face a power hitter with the game on the line, you might walk him. You can't do that with Bonds. If you walk him, that's like giving up a double, because he's going to steal second base."

Many people say that Barry has been the best player in baseball in the 1990's. He has won three MVP trophies and eight Gold Glove awards. But Barry doesn't display his awards around his house, in Los Altos Hills, California. "If you walk in the front door you will not see a trophy," says Barry.

Part of the reason for that is that Barry remembers going to Willie Mays' house as a kid and not seeing baseball memorabilia everywhere. It was a fun place to relax and get away from the pressures of being a major league baseball player.

> **"He's the best player I've ever seen. For as long as he's kept it up, there's been nobody like him."**
> **— Mark Grace, first baseman, Chicago Cubs**

"Willie had the most fun house I've ever seen," says Barry. "There was a swimming pool and a pool room, and I remember having the best time there."

Barry is still having a good time — at home and as a ballplayer. Even though he's in his mid-30s, he remains one of the best players in the game. Only nagging injuries kept him out of the 1999 All-Star Game.

"I just love the game," says Barry. "And I will keep playing it until they kick me out!" ★

LARRY WALKER

Outfielder, Colorado Rockies
Height: 6' 3"   **Weight: 237 pounds**
Bats: Left   **Throws: Right**
Birth Date: December 1, 1966
Birth Place: Maple
Ridge, British
Columbia, Canada
Entered Majors: 1989

Many people believe that rightfielder Larry Walker of the Colorado Rockies is the best player in the National League. "He does things that no one else can do," says pitcher Curt Schilling of the Philadelphia Phillies.

But would you believe that when Larry was in high school, he barely knew how

With stats like this man has, he should be named Larry Hitter!

to play baseball? It's true. Larry grew up in Maple Ridge, British Columbia, in Canada. He enjoyed playing hockey much more than baseball. "I'm cuckoo about hockey," says Larry.

Larry's high school didn't even have a baseball team. He played the sport occasionally during the summer. But even with limited playing opportunities, it became clear that Larry had a lot of natural talent for baseball. When his attempts at a hockey career went nowhere, Larry got more serious about baseball.

Larry's first season as a pro ballplayer came in 1985, in the Montreal Expos' minor league system. He could hit the ball far — but only when he hit it. "I swung at two balls in a row that bounced in front of home plate," Larry says with a laugh. "And I'd never seen a slider before, or a curveball. I was very raw." At one point, Larry got so frustrated at failing at baseball that he almost quit the game and went home to take take another shot at hockey.

Good thing he didn't! Larry stuck with baseball and worked hard to improve. Once he began learning more about the game, his great athletic ability started kicking in. He reached the major leagues in 1989.

FAST FACTS

☆ Became the first Canadian to win the National League MVP award, in 1997
☆ Has won two N.L. batting titles
☆ Prefers wearing shorts and a T-shirt to a jacket and tie. "I have lots of nice clothes," says Larry. "I just don't wear them."

Three years later, he blossomed into a .300 hitter. Since joining the Colorado Rockies in 1995, his offensive numbers have been stunning.

In 1997, Larry won the National League MVP award, after hitting .366 and leading the league with 49 home runs. In 1998, he won his first batting title with a .363 average. He added a second batting title in 1999, finishing with a terrific .379 average. He had 37 homers and 115 runs batted in for the season as well.

In addition, Larry has won four Gold Gloves for his great defense in rightfield. He really can do it all. "He's as good as it gets," says his teammate Dante Bichette. "You drop your jaw at the things he can do on a baseball field."

> "Larry isn't just a great hitter. He's the best base runner I've ever seen."
> — Jim Leyland, manager, Colorado Rockies

Not bad for a player who barely knew which end of the bat to hold as a kid, eh?

"My story shows how far someone can come in the game," says Larry. "It was really hard for me, but I never gave up. Keep fighting, and you never know what can happen. If kids think they're not good enough, that they're never going to make it, look at me." ★

Honorable Mention

With so many awesome stars in the major leagues, selecting just 22 as All-Stars is not only tough, it's just not enough. We picked our starting lineups and then looked around.

What about dominating pitchers like Greg Maddux and Roger "the Rocket" Clemens? What about a dynamic duo of young shortstops, Derek Jeter and Nomar Garciaparra?

Clearly something had to be done. That something became this Honorable Mention chapter. We made space for Greg and Roger, for Derek and Nomar. We pitched in another Cy Young-winning pitcher, Tom Glavine.

While we were at it, we made space for unhittable young closer Billy Wagner. Then we added super-slugger Jeff Bagwell. For even more pop at the plate, we added a pair of outstanding outfielders: Bernie Williams and Shawn Green.

You might feel that some of these talented players should be in our starting lineup, instead of the players we picked. That's fine with us. Part of the fun of sports is debating which players are the very best! ★

GREG MADDUX

Pitcher, Atlanta Braves **Throws: Right**
Bats: Right **Entered Majors: 1986**
Height: 6' Weight: 185 pounds
Born: April 14, 1966, in San Angelo, Texas

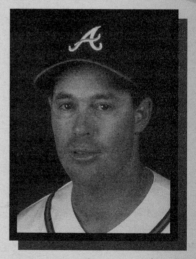

Greg Maddux may be the best pitcher of the 1990's. Greg won the National League Cy Young Award four years in a row, from 1992 to 1995. Greg also led the N.L. in earned run average four times in the 1990's. He's a great fielder, too, and had won nine straight Gold Glove awards through 1998.

With his pinpoint control and smart pitch selection, Greg carves up opposing lineups like Thanksgiving turkeys. Even the best hitters around don't like to face him. "When he's on, one-for-four is a great day," says San Diego Padre hitting star Tony Gwynn. ★

ROGER CLEMENS

Pitcher, New York Yankees   Throws: Right
Bats: Right   Entered Majors: 1984
Height: 6' 4"   Weight: 230 pounds
Born: August 4, 1962, in Dayton, Ohio

When Roger Clemens of the New York Yankees is on the pitcher's mound, he's about as intense as can be. Former teammate Charlie O'Brien once said, "You can almost see smoke coming out of his nose!"

Roger throws smoke, too. His awesome fastball has been clocked as high as 97 miles per hour and has earned him the nickname The Rocket.

Through 1999, The Rocket led the American League in most strikeouts in a season five times. He had also captured five A.L. Cy Young Awards — more than any other pitcher in history!   ★

TOM GLAVINE

Pitcher, Atlanta Braves　　**Throws: Left**
Bats: Left　　**Entered Majors: 1987**
Height: 6'　　**Weight: 185 pounds**
Born: March 25, 1966, in Concord, Massachusetts

Pitcher Tom Glavine of the Atlanta Braves just does not feel pressure. Flash back to 1995. It is two hours before Tom is to start Game 6 of the World Series against the Cleveland Indians. Tom is taking a 45-minute nap in the clubhouse!

"I wanted to relax," said Tom. That night, Tom pitched a one-hit shutout, and the Braves won the World Series. "It is an awesome feeling," he said.

Speaking of awesome, Tom has won two National League Cy Young Awards, in 1991 and 1998. He has also had 20 or more victories in a season four times through 1999. ★

BILLY WAGNER

Pitcher, Houston Astros   **Throws: Left**
Bats: Left   Entered Majors: 1996
Height: 5' 11"   Weight: 180 pounds
Born: July 25, 1971, in Tannersville, Virginia

Billy Wagner is one of the shortest pitchers in the major leagues. He is officially listed at 5-foot-11 (that might be *stretching* things a bit . . .). But the Houston Astros' left-handed closer also throws one of the meanest fastballs around. His pitches have been clocked as high as 100 miles per hour on the radar gun.

"I love throwing the ball as hard as I can," says Billy. "I just say to the batter, 'Here it is, try to hit it.' "

They try, but they don't hit it often. Want proof? In 1999, Billy had more saves (39) than hits allowed (35)!   ★

JEFF BAGWELL

First Baseman, Houston Astros   Bats: Right
Throws: Right   Entered Majors: 1991
Height: 6'   Weight: 195 pounds
Born: May 27, 1968, in Boston, Massachusetts

Houston Astro first baseman Jeff Bagwell has one of the strangest batting stances in the major leagues. He squats down at home plate and spreads his legs wide apart. Jeff's stance may look odd, but it gets the job done!

Through 1999, Jeff had a career batting average of .304. He had slammed an average of 35 homers per year over the previous six seasons.

Jeff's great play helped Houston make the playoffs in 1997, 1998, and 1999. "He's our main man," says Astro manager Larry Dierker.   ★

DEREK JETER

Shortstop, New York Yankees   **Bats: Right**
Throws: Right   **Entered Majors: 1995**
Height: 6' 3"   **Weight: 195 pounds**
Born: June 26, 1974, in Pequannock, New Jersey

New York Yankee shortstop Derek Jeter isn't just a great young player — he's a great player regardless of age. He had a .308 batting average in his first three seasons and helped the Yankees win two World Series.

Even though Derek only turned 25 in 1999, he is also recognized for his leadership. "If people want to view me as a leader because I play hard and give 100 percent, that's fine with me," says Derek. "But it's not something I sit and think about too much. I just go out and play and try to get better." ★

NOMAR GARCIAPARRA

**Shortstop, Boston Red Sox   Bats: Right
Throws: Right   Entered Majors: 1996
Height: 6'   Weight: 180 pounds
Born: July 23, 1973, in Whittier, California**

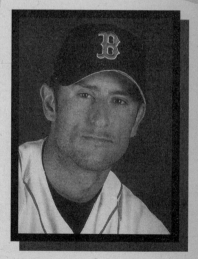

Boston Red Sox shortstop Nomar Garciaparra is very superstitious. He walks down into the dugout one step at a time. And when he's in the batter's box, he's always tugging on his batting gloves and tapping his toes.

"I just like to be ready," says Nomar.

Nomar is *more* than ready! He won the A.L. Rookie of the Year award in 1997, when he hit .306, belted 30 homers, and drove in 98 runs. In 1998, Nomar batted .323, with 35 homers and 122 runs batted in! He continued to improve in 1999 and won the A.L. batting title with a .357 average. ★

BERNIE WILLIAMS

Outfielder, New York Yankees   **Bats: Both**
Throws: Right   **Entered Majors: 1991**
Height: 6' 2"   **Weight: 205 pounds**
Born: September 13, 1968, in San Juan, Puerto Rico

Centerfielder Bernie Williams of the New York Yankees likes to relax in the clubhouse by strumming his electric guitar. But he makes his sweetest music on the field.

Bernie won the 1998 American League batting title with a .339 average. He is also a fantastic fielder. He used his defensive skills to snag Gold Gloves in 1997 and 1998. Bernie was one of the biggest reasons the Yankees won the 1996 and 1998 World Series.

"He can help you win in a lot of different ways," says Williams' teammate, slugger Paul O'Neill.   ★

80

SHAWN GREEN

Outfielder, Toronto Blue Jays   **Bats: Left**

Throws: Left   **Entered Majors: 1993**

Height: 6' 4"   **Weight: 200 pounds**

Born: November 10, 1972, in Des Plaines, Illinois

Toronto Blue Jay outfielder Shawn Green has one of the sweetest swings in baseball. He keeps the bat level and always follows through with perfect balance.

Shawn learned his swing as a kid. A friend's father bought a pitching machine but had no room for it in his backyard. Shawn started hitting every day off the machine.

All that practice has paid off! Shawn smacked 35 homers in 1998. He belted 42 more in 1999. "I kind of surprised myself by hitting so many home runs in 1998," Shawn said. "But now I kind of expect it."

So should you!   ★

Stars of the Future

So far, you've been reading about the very best players of today. But what about tomorrow? Which of baseball's bright young stars will become the All-Stars of the future?

Well, we don't have a crystal ball, but we do watch *a lot* of baseball, talk to *a lot* of players and coaches, and pour over *a lot* of statistics. Add 'em all up, and you get our seven best guesses. We think these players have the talent, skill, and attitude to become superstars.

Slugger Sean Casey looks as though he has the swing to start winning batting titles. Gritty catcher Jason Kendall has a powerful bat and surprising speed. Jeff Weaver's fastball is just plain nasty. Third baseman Scott Rolen is a big guy who will be putting up big numbers for years to come.

In the outfield, we have three very different players with one thing in common: big-time talent. Carlos Beltran is a clutch hitter, Vladimir Guerrero is a powerful slugger, and Andruw Jones is a jet-powered defensive wizard.

Look for all of these stars to light up the major leagues for years to come! ★

SEAN CASEY

First Baseman, Cincinnati Reds   Bats: Left
Throws: Right   Entered Majors: 1997
Height: 6' 4"   Weight: 215 pounds
Born: July 2, 1974, in Willingboro, New Jersey

Reds' slugger Sean Casey was hit in the eye with a ball early in the 1998 season. He broke a bone near his eye. Sean had to have surgery to correct his vision. He wondered whether his career was over.

After a lot of hard work and a few tune-up games in the minors, Sean made it back to the big leagues five weeks later. He had three hits in his first game back! He followed up those hits by batting .332 with 25 homers in 1999.

"I feel very lucky after my accident," says Sean. *He* feels lucky, but pitchers don't!   ★

JASON KENDALL

Catcher, Pittsburgh Pirates   Bats: Right
Throws: Right   Entered Majors: 1996
Height: 6'   Weight: 193 pounds
Born: June 26, 1974, in San Diego, California

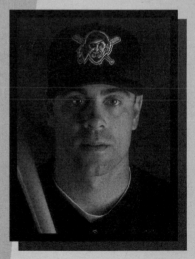

It's hard to find a major league player with a dirtier uniform than Jason Kendall's. Pittsburgh's scrappy catcher picks up loads of dirt while scrambling to block pitches at the plate and diving headfirst when he's running the bases.

Jason has turned all that hustle — and all that dirt — into big-league success. In 1998, he batted .327 and stole 26 bases, the most stolen bases ever by a National League catcher.

"The day that I can't get up and bust my tail on a daily basis, that's the day I will retire," says Jason. "I'm gonna try my hardest until they rip the uniform off me."   ★

JEFF WEAVER

Pitcher, Detroit Tigers   **Throws: Right**
Bats: Right   **Entered Majors: 1999**
Height: 6' 5"   **Weight: 200 pounds**
Born: August 22, 1976, in Northridge, California

Pitcher Jeff Weaver of the Detroit Tigers reached the major leagues almost as fast as one of his 92-mile-per-hour heaters reaches home plate. He started winning even faster! Jeff pitched just 31 career innings in the minor leagues before he was promoted to the big leagues in April 1999. In his first 10 starts for Detroit, he won six games, lost only three, and had a 3.00 earned run average.

Batters were really blown away by Jeff and the wicked fastball he throws from all sorts of arm angles. "That guy's nasty," says slugger Frank Thomas of the Chicago White Sox.   ★

SCOTT ROLEN

Third Baseman, Philadelphia Phillies   Bats: Right
Throws: Right   Entered Majors: 1996
Height: 6' 4"   Weight: 225 pounds
Born: April 4, 1975, in Jasper, Indiana

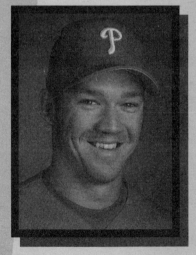

Scott Rolen of the Phillies bashes 25 home runs and steals 15 bases per year. But the first word that his manager uses to describe him isn't slugger or competitor, it's nice. Scott says "Yes, sir" and "No, sir" and "Thank you." He signs hundreds and hundreds of autographs for fans.

"What a nice kid," says Phillies' manager Terry Francona.

Scott might be nice off the field, but he's a hard-charging warrior on it. He was the 1997 National League Rookie of the Year. He followed that up by driving in 110 runs in 1998.

For Phillie fans, that's *very* nice.   ★

CARLOS BELTRAN

Outfielder, Kansas City Royals   Bats: Both
Throws: Right   Entered Majors: 1998
Height: 6'   Weight: 175 pounds
Born: April 24, 1977, in Manati, Puerto Rico

Carlos Beltran of the Kansas City Royals is one of the best young players in baseball. He proved it in 1999 by hitting .293, with 22 homers and 27 stolen bases.

The red-hot rookie also proved that he's cool under pressure. On July 2, he hit a three-run double in the 10th inning that beat the Cleveland Indians. Four days later, he beat the Chicago White Sox with a 10th-inning single.

"I don't feel any pressure," says Carlos. "I like those situations."

Carlos isn't just good, he's also *cool*.   ★

ANDRUW JONES

Outfielder, Atlanta Braves   **Bats: Right**
Throws: Right   **Entered Majors: 1996**
Height: 6' 1"   **Weight: 185 pounds**
Born: April 23, 1977, in Willemstad, Curaçao

Atlanta centerfielder Andruw Jones hits a lot of home runs and steals a lot of bases. But what really makes him stand out is his defensive ability.

Andruw uses his blazing speed to track down and catch fly balls that look like sure doubles or triples when they leave the bat. "He's a highlight film," says Brave pitcher Tom Glavine.

In 1998, Andruw won the first of what will probably be many Gold Glove awards for his outstanding defense. He was just 21 years old — which made him the youngest National League outfielder ever to win a Gold Glove.   ★

VLADIMIR GUERRERO

Outfielder, Montreal Expos   **Bats: Right**
Throws: Right   **Entered Majors: 1996**
Height: 6' 3"   **Weight: 205 pounds**
Born: February 9, 1976, in the Dominican Republic

Young Expos' outfielder Vladimir Guerrero is already one of the most talked-about hitters in the major leagues.

"That guy is awesome," says Philadephia Phillies' pitcher Curt Schilling.

Vladimir exploded on the scene in 1998. He hit .324, with 38 home runs and 109 runs batted in. He continued his fireworks in 1999, finishing with a .316 batting average, 42 home runs, and 131 RBIs.

"I always knew I had the talent," says Vladimir. "I feel like a better hitter each day."

In other words, get ready for more fireworks!   ★

Tribute

More than any other sport, baseball is rooted in tradition. Baseball has always celebrated its past while it has moved into the future.

This book has celebrated the brightest stars of today and of tomorrow. Now it's time to take a look at two stars who have already secured a place in baseball history. Cal Ripken, Junior, and Tony Gwynn are not only classy competitors, they are sure-fire future Hall of Famers.

Cal is a baseball warrior who didn't miss a game for 16 straight seasons. His streak of playing in 2,632 consecutive games ranks among the greatest individual accomplishments in *all* of sports history.

Tony is the greatest pure hitter of his generation — and one of the greatest of all time. In 1999, he topped the 3,000 career hit mark. Not too many players even get close to that!

Surprisingly, both of these legends have spent their entire careers with one team: Cal with the Baltimore Orioles and Tony with the San Diego Padres.

Here is our tribute to two of the game's greatest.   ★

CAL RIPKEN, JUNIOR

Third Baseman, Baltimore Orioles
Height: 6' 4"   **Weight: 220 pounds**
Bats: Right   **Throws: Right**
Birth Date: August 24, 1960
Birth Place: Havre de Grace, Maryland
Entered Majors: 1981

Everyone knows that Cal Ripken, Junior, of the Baltimore Orioles is a hero to millions of kids. But did you know that he's also a hero to many major leaguers? "Most players today grew up watching Cal and have tried to imitate him," says Alex Rodriguez of the Seattle Mariners. "He always does everything with class." Says Shawn Green of the Toronto Blue Jays: "I've always liked him. I got his autograph when I was thirteen or fourteen."

Cal is best known for playing in 2,632 straight games. That set a record that might never be broken. Cal didn't miss a game for 16 seasons! Players still are in awe of that. "That streak is just about the most amazing thing that can be done in baseball — in all of sports," says Shawn.

Cal has won two American League MVP awards. He was one of the best shortstops in baseball history before moving to third base two years ago. But Cal is just as nice as he is talented. He often signs autographs for hours after games. An organization that he and his wife started, called the Kelly and Cal Ripken, Junior, Foundation, supports literacy programs for adults and recreational and health programs for kids in the Baltimore area.

"When I was just learning the game, I watched how Cal carried himself on and off the field. I decided, 'That's

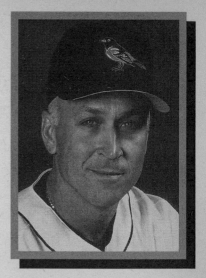

Built to last: Cal is baseball's all-time Iron Man.

FAST FACTS

☆ Played in 2,632 consecutive games, the major league record
☆ Won American League MVP awards in 1983 and 1991
☆ Played 95 straight games at shortstop without an error (1990)
☆ Loves to play basketball and has a full-sized court in his home

the way to do it,' " says Chipper Jones of the Atlanta Braves. "There's no better role model in baseball."

Cal's own role model was his father, Cal, Senior. His dad was a longtime minor league manager and instructor for the Orioles. He also managed the O's from 1987-88. He taught Cal everything about the game.

Cal senior died in March 1999. This made the early part of the 1999 season difficult for Cal, Junior. Then in April, a back injury put him on the disabled list for the first time in his career.

"There are a lot of different things that happened to me that I didn't have experience for or hadn't prepared for," Cal said. "But you deal with them and learn from them."

Some people thought Cal might retire. But this baseball warrior came back as strong as ever. He even went 6-for-6 with two home runs in one game in June. He finished with an impressive .340 average and 18 homers.

"I plan on playing for a long time," Cal said. For all the people out there who consider Cal their hero, that's very good news. ★

"Cal has everything you could want in a player — a great bat and a great glove."
— Alex Rodriguez, shortstop, Seattle Mariners

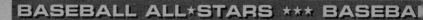

TONY GWYNN

Outfielder, San Diego Padres
Height: 5' 11"   Weight: 220 pounds
Bats: Left   Throws: Left
Birth Date: May 9, 1960
Birth Place: Los Angeles, California
Entered Majors: 1982

You have probably heard of pitching machines. They throw pitch after pitch after pitch. Well, San Diego Padre right-fielder Tony Gwynn is a *hitting* machine. He gets hit after hit after hit! Tony has won eight National League batting titles. He captured four straight from 1994 (when he hit .394!) through 1997.

The hits kept on coming in 1999. In a game against the Montreal Expos on August 6, Tony collected career hit number 3,000. Tony smacked a single in his first at-bat of the game to become just the 22nd major leaguer to get 3,000 hits. Then he added three more hits on the night, for good measure!

Tony has spent his entire 18-season career with San Diego. People wonder how he has been able to stay so good for so long. That's easy. He watches a lot of television. Well, not really television; he watches video, as in videotapes of his at-bats. Tony watches tapes of himself hitting. He tries to make sure he's doing everything right, and he tries to see what pitchers are doing to try to get him out.

"Without video, I don't think I'd still be here," says Tony. He takes his video viewing very seriously. On every road trip, Tony carries a suitcase that has three different video machines, a 10-inch monitor, and lots of tapes. The bag weighs 35 pounds!

"I don't look at it as work," says Tony. "I just look at it as getting ready to do what I have to do."

Tony should start getting ready for baseball's ultimate honor: getting inducted into the Hall of Fame. He's a shoo-in when he becomes eligible. And there's a good chance he will videotape the induction ceremony! ★

Tony is a big hit in San Diego.

FAST FACTS

☆ Joined baseball's "3,000-hits club" on August 6, 1999
☆ Won eight National League batting titles, between 1984 and 1997
☆ Was a star basketball player at San Diego State University and was drafted by the Clippers (10th round, 1981)

WANT TO HAVE MORE FUN!

WITH SPORTS ILLUSTRATED FOR KIDS?

◎ **GET A FREE TRIAL ISSUE** of SPORTS ILLUSTRATED FOR KIDS **magazine**. Each monthly issue is jam-packed with awesome athletes, super-sized photos, cool sports facts, comics, games, and jokes!

Ask your mom or dad to call and order your free trial issue today! The phone number is 1-800-732-5080.

◎ **PLUG IN TO** www.sikids.com. That's the S.I. FOR KIDS' website on the internet. You'll find great games, free fantasy leagues, sports news, trivia quizzes, and more. (Tell your mom and dad to check out www.sportsparents.com, too.)

◎ **CHECK OUT** S.I. FOR KIDS Weekly in the comic section of many newspapers. It has lots of cool photos, stories, and puzzles from the Number 1 sports magazine for kids!

◎ **LOOK FOR** more S.I. FOR KIDS books. They make reading **fun!**